For Ernie

On these pages you will find

ORCHARD BOOKS
96 Leonard Street, London EC2A 4RH
Orchard Books Australia
14 Mars Road, Lane Cove, NSW 2066
First published in Great Britain 1990
First paperback publication 1992
Text and illustrations copyright © Venice Shone 1990
1 85213 225 6 (hardback)
1 85213 359 7 (paperback)
A CIP catalogue record for this book is available
from the British Library.
Printed in Belgium

Wheels

VENICE SHONE

ORCHARD BOOKS

baby wheels

pram

2

play wheels

roller skates

tricycle

skateboard

3

bicycle wheels

bicycle

motorbike wheels

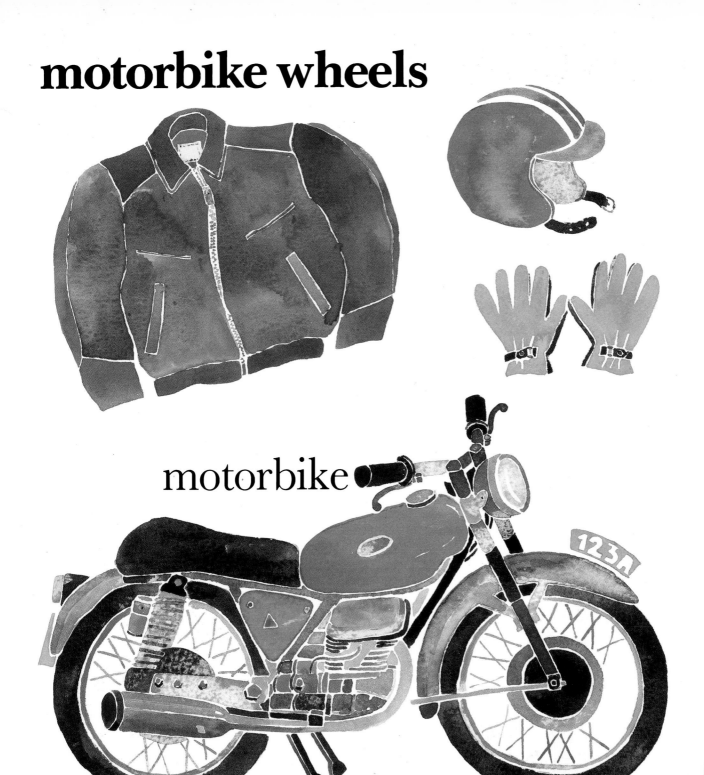

motorbike

5

6

racing wheels

racing car

car wheels

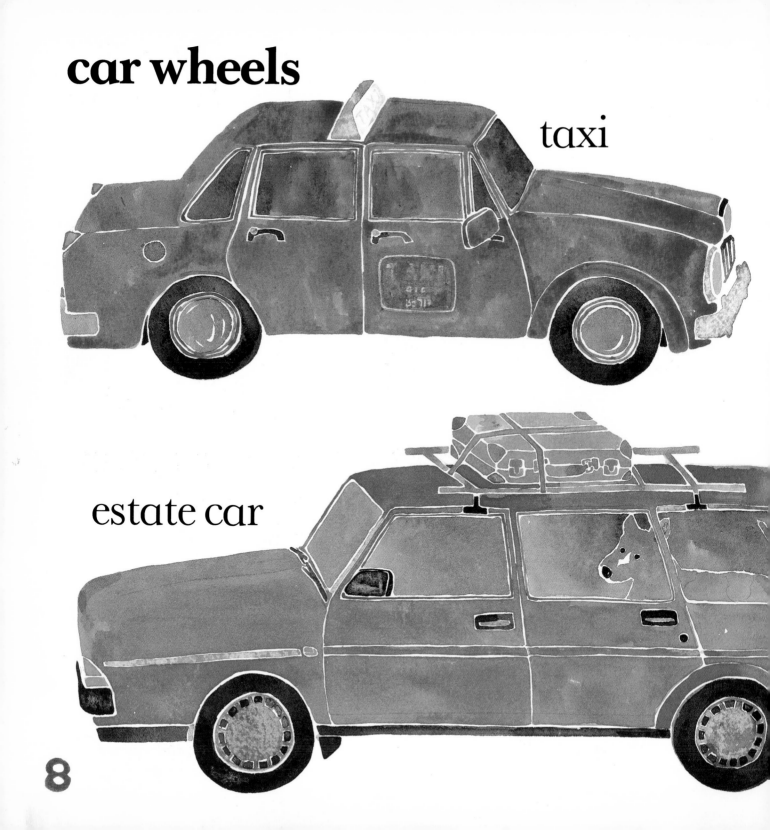

taxi

estate car

8

wedding car

learner-driver car

DRIVING SCHOOL

wheels on the bus

school bus

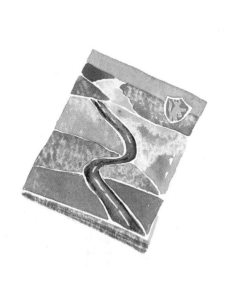

10

Bus

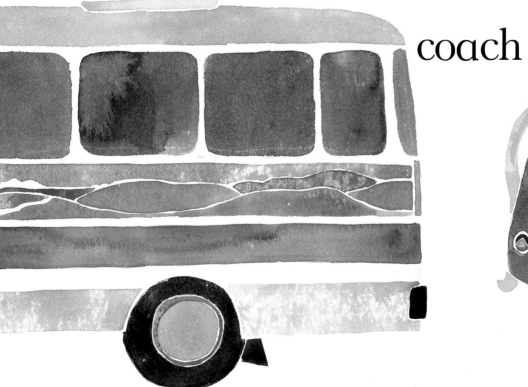

coach

baker's van

removal van

laundry van

florist's van

police car

ambulance

14

emergency wheels

fire engine

dump truck

wheelbarrow

16

working wheels

cement mixer

away-day wheels

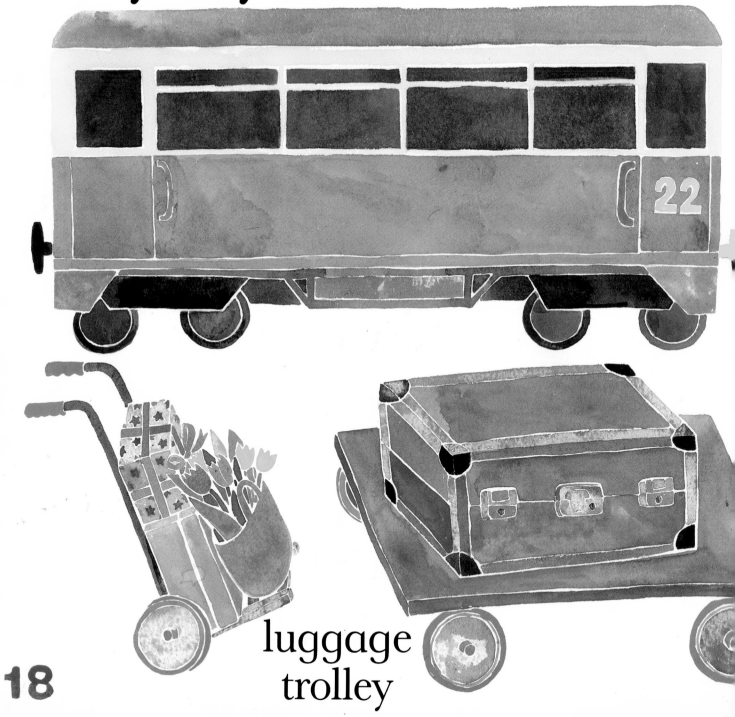

22

luggage
trolley

18

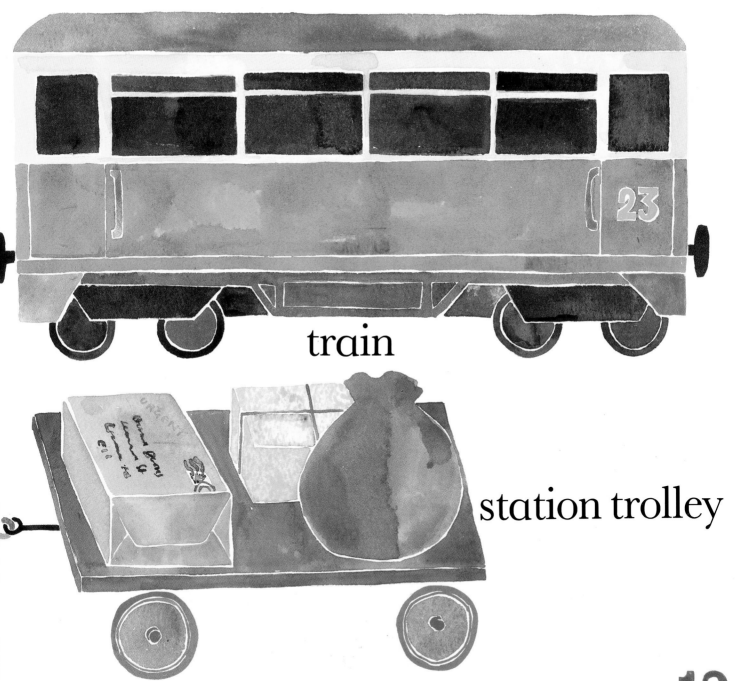

train

station trolley

19

20

up, up and away wheels

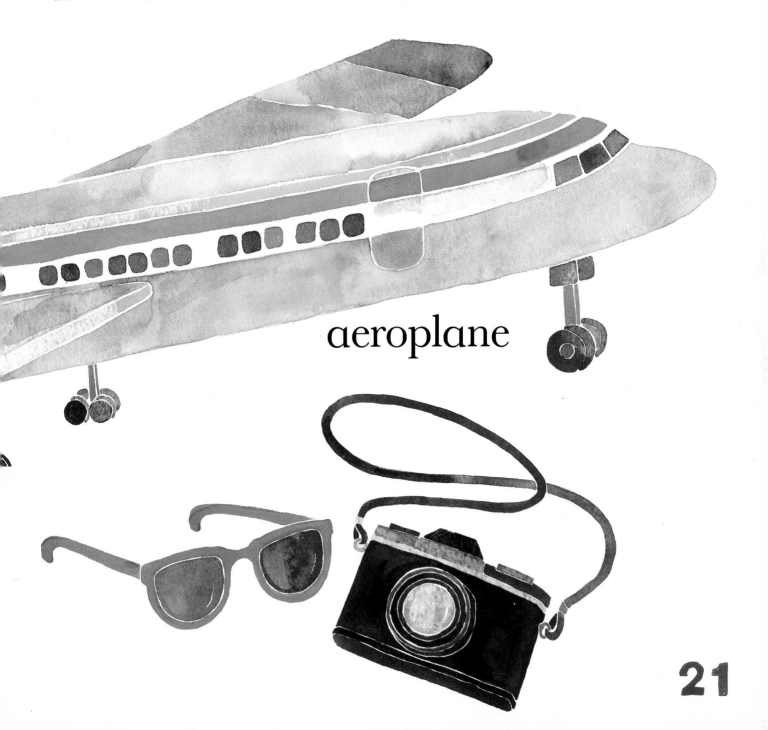

aeroplane

21

holiday wheels

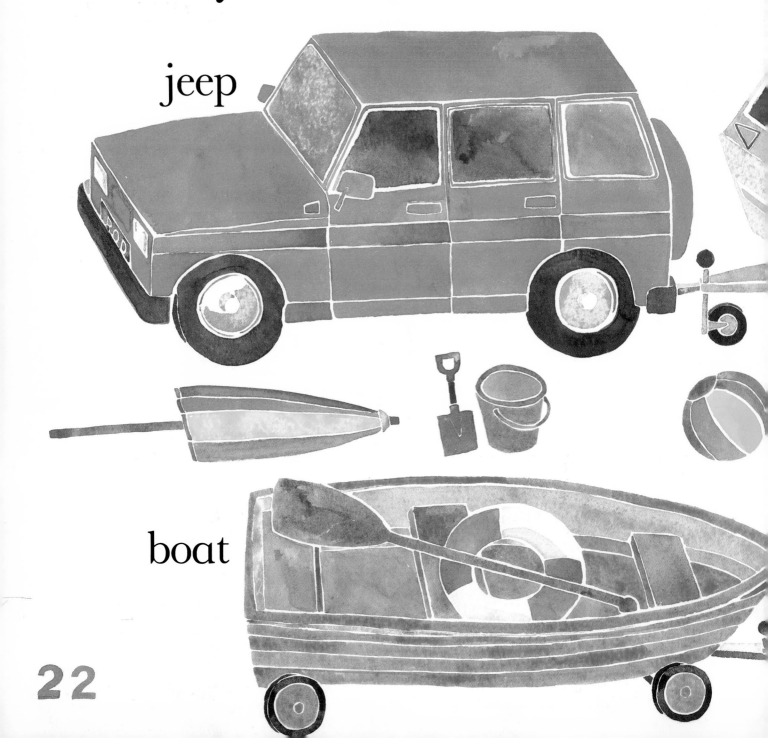

jeep

boat

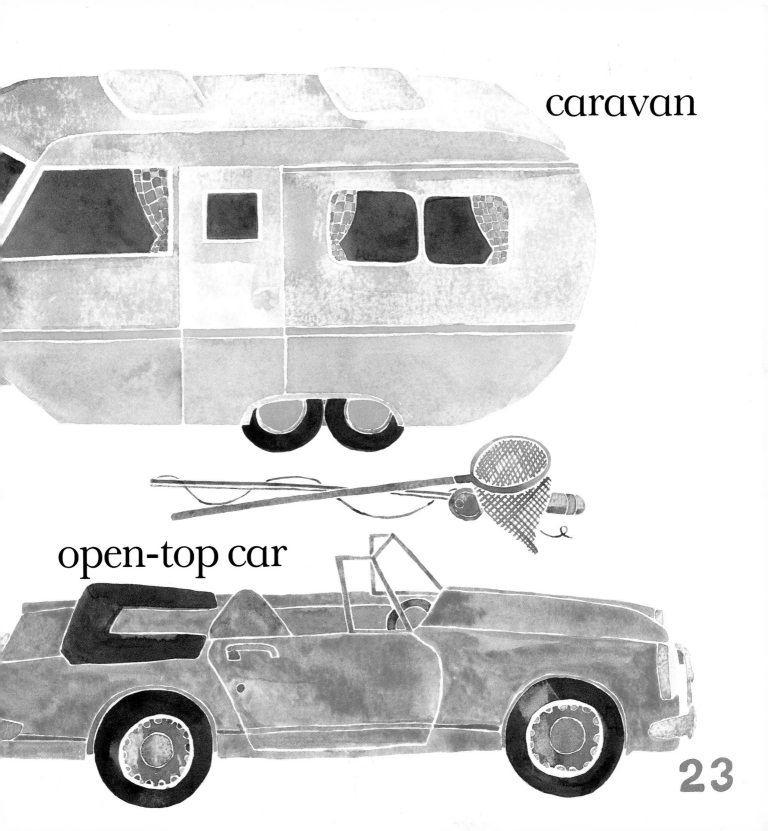

caravan

open-top car

23

wheels on wheels

car transporter

25

For Ernie

On these pages you will find

ORCHARD BOOKS
96 Leonard Street, London EC2A 4RH
Orchard Books Australia
14 Mars Road, Lane Cove, NSW 2066
First published in Great Britain 1990
First paperback publication 1992
Text and illustrations copyright © Venice Shone 1990
1 85213 225 6 (hardback)
1 85213 359 7 (paperback)
A CIP catalogue record for this book is available
from the British Library.
Printed in Belgium

Wheels

VENICE SHONE

ORCHARD BOOKS

baby wheels

pram

2

play wheels

roller skates

tricycle

skateboard

3

bicycle wheels

bicycle

motorbike wheels

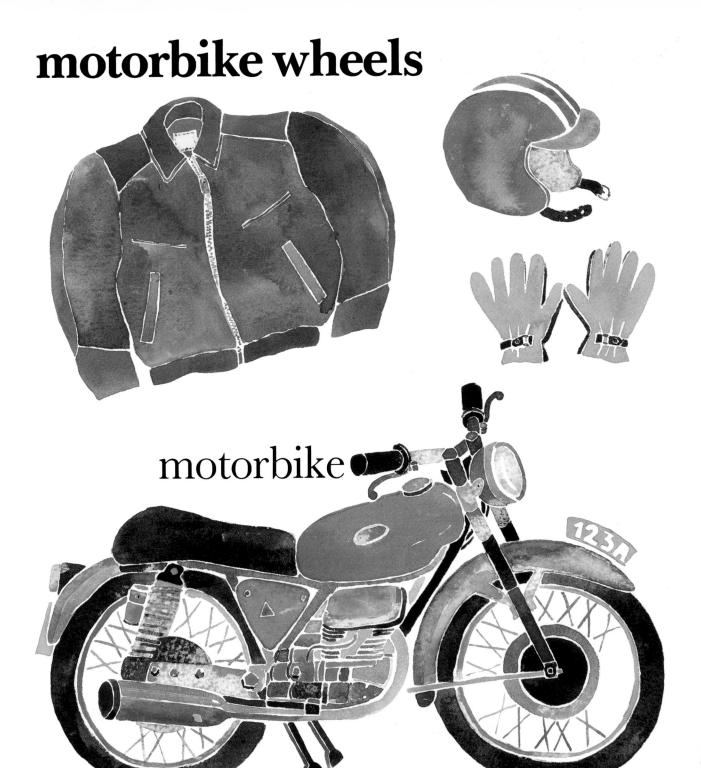

motorbike

6

racing wheels

racing car

car wheels

taxi

estate car

8

wedding car

LERNIE
L 123
986

learner-driver
car

DRIVING
SCHOOL

9

wheels on the bus

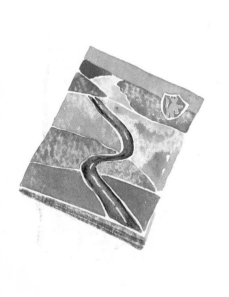

school bus

Bus

coach

11

baker's van

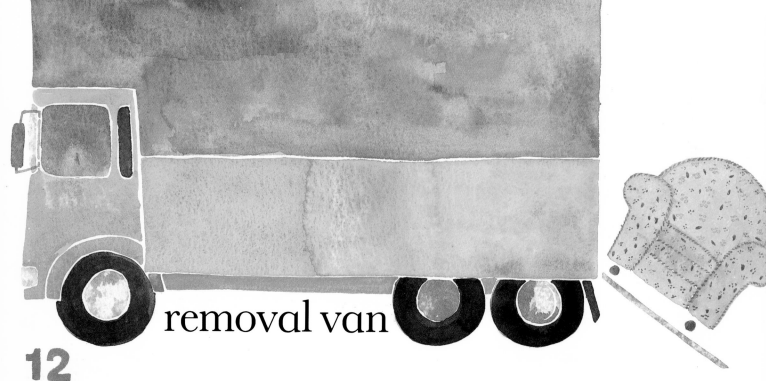

removal van

laundry van

florist's van

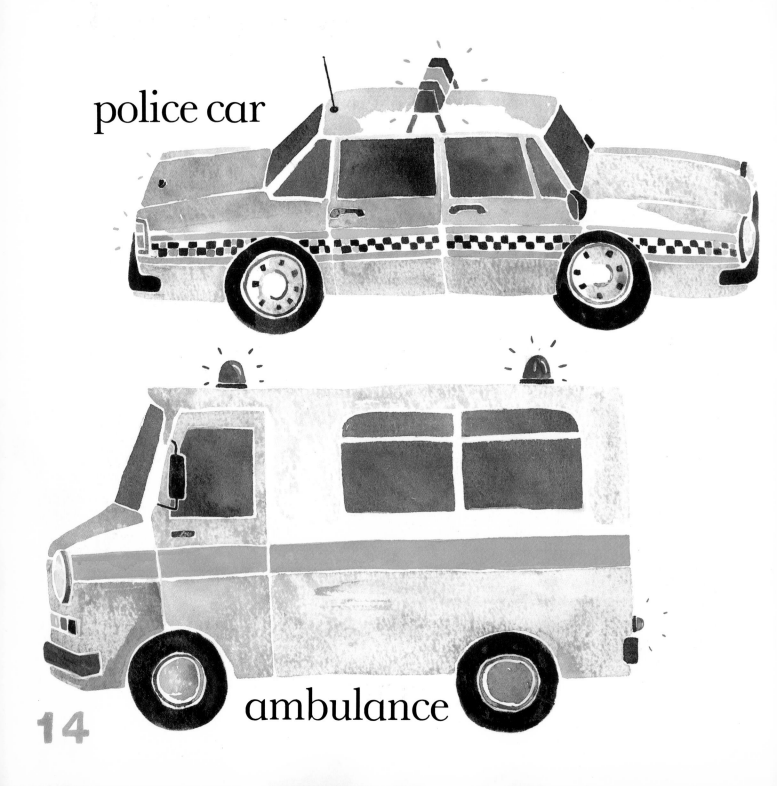

police car

ambulance

14

emergency wheels

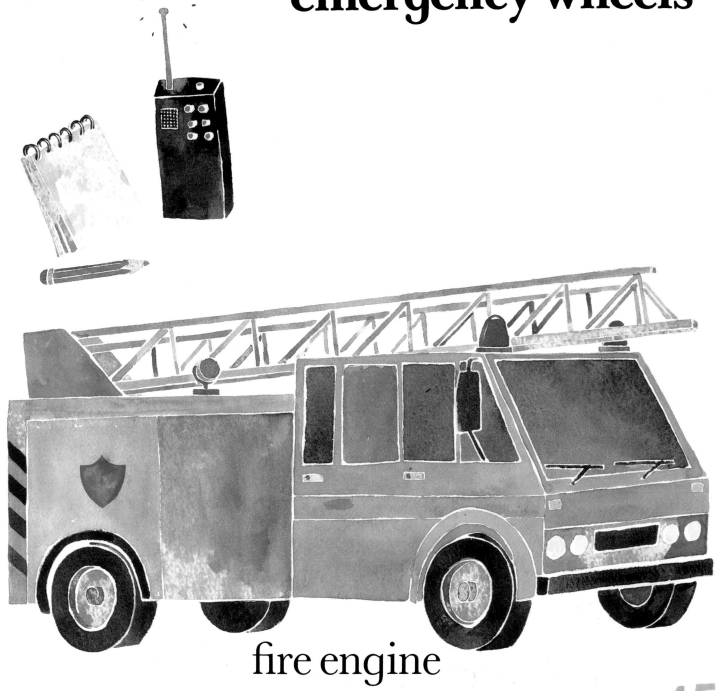

fire engine

dump truck

wheelbarrow

16

working wheels

cement mixer

17

away-day wheels

22

luggage
trolley

18

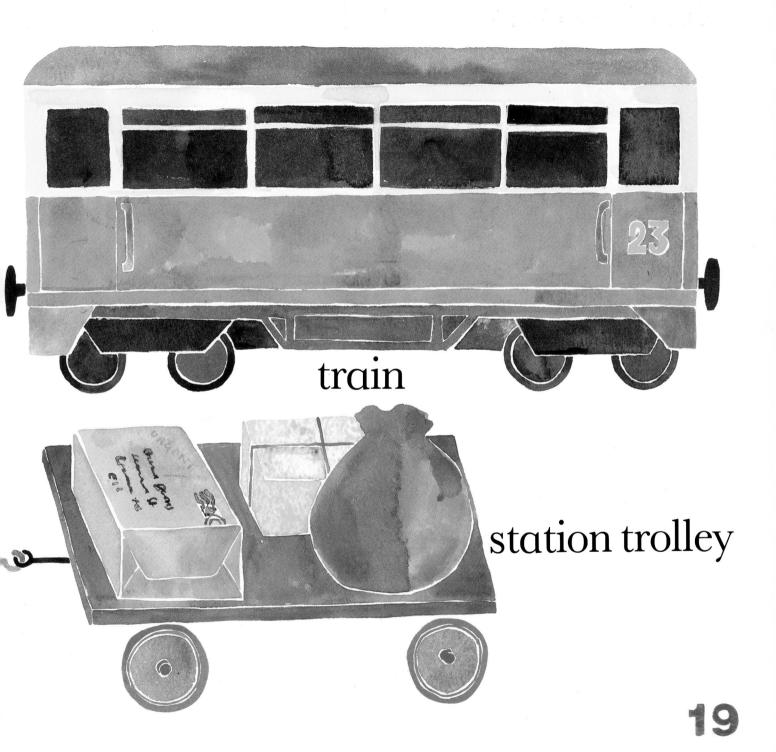

train

station trolley

19

20

up, up and away wheels

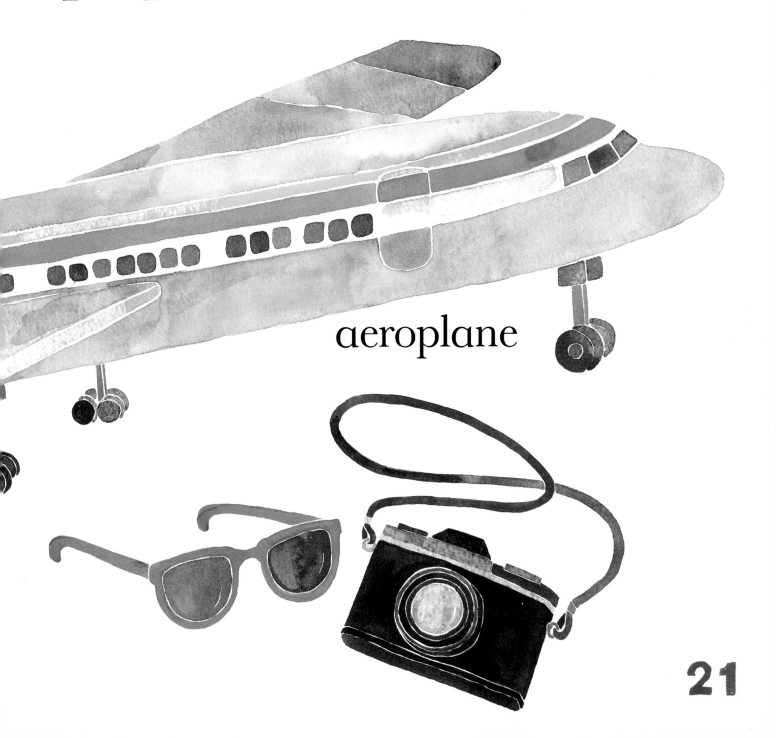

aeroplane

21

holiday wheels

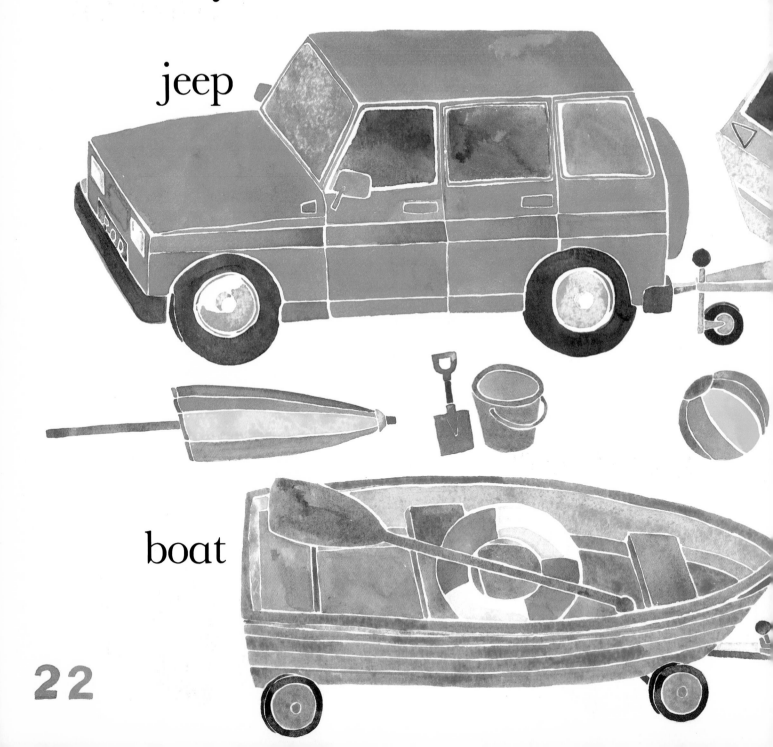

jeep

boat

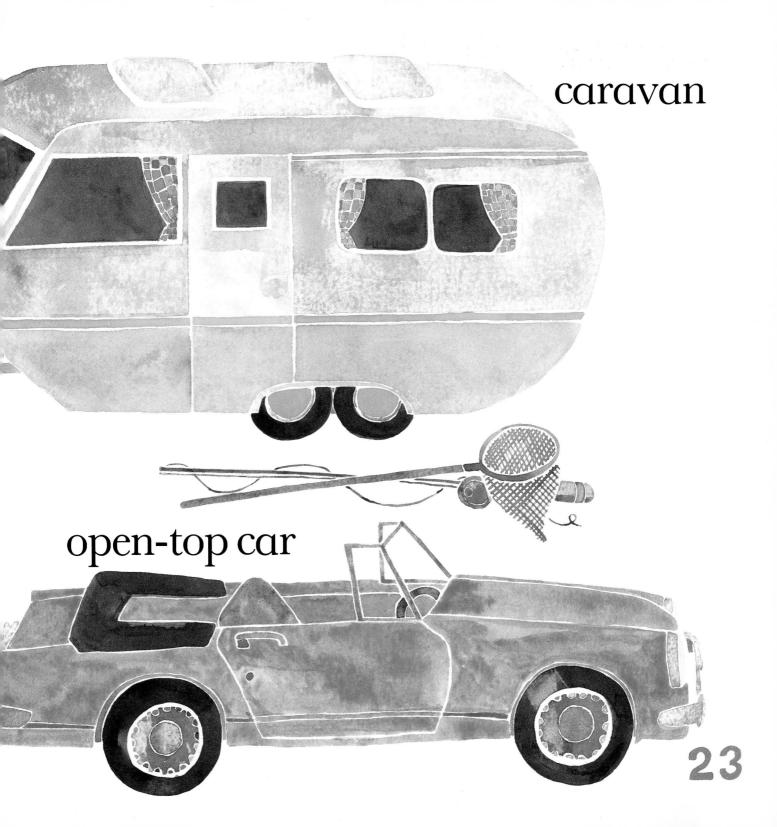

caravan

open-top car

23

wheels on wheels

car transporter

25